UNBRIDLED

MARIA K CRAWFORD

# UNBRIDLED

Maria K Crawford

www.mariakcrawford.com

Designed by Harsh Yellow Creative

To all those
Who have swam in my waters
Rough, calm, or otherwise
You are each a part of me
And therefore
A part of this book, too

*Dedication*

MARIA K CRAWFORD

These poems were written to keep me standing. Scribbled in notebooks that sometimes I couldn't even read. On a never-made bed in the dark. On the roof of my very favorite apartment in my very least favorite town. In the grass beside wildflowers and weeds. With tears and love in my eyes, and sometimes both, during a time when no one could listen even if they tried. Because there was no way to explain what was happening. No guide.

And so the paper listened. And it made sense of things. As I fell out of love and too quickly back in, I learned the one I needed to love most was *me*.

That story has reached your hands, on today of all days, for a reason that I don't know. But I am so glad it did. And I am so glad you're here. Love is tricky. Sticky. Beautiful and awful and free and captivating.

And so are you, my reader.
And so am I.

*To my reader*

MARIA K CRAWFORD

## CONTENTS

PART ONE

Harbor

**I wish I could read it like a book**

**Everything you did**

**To make me**

**Never cry over you**

*Now I can*

Sitting here

Alone in this apartment

The world having spun

At a thousand miles per hour

To get me here

Back where I started

Almost like it was a dream

I'm waking up now

With nothing left

But tears in my eyes

I thought the song was perfect

*You're a lighthouse*

Sounded

So right

How is it possible

To feel

Opposites

In such magnitude

Wishing

I was back there

With you

When, in truth,

I hated every minute

I am

Legitimately

Terrified

Of what I've done

So much

That I feel

I may not live through it

What worth

Do promises have?

We mean them

When we make them

Until we don't

The unfulfilled desire

To be someone's

Everything

Where they see you

As a person

Put on this earth

To nourish

Every piece

Of their soul

Has to be the most pain

I will ever feel

And maybe won't ever

Let go of

I should have known

As soon as I noticed

It used to feel right

They tell me

To get myself together

How could I

Fall apart

So easily?

I ask them,

*What am I supposed to do*

*When I'm suffocating?*

*Pull tighter*

*Or let go?*

I always said

Love is a choice

We chose fear

Lost

Not without you

But without myself

I can't cry

If I cry, it's real

And this can't be real

Will they all end this way

With love

Burning out

At the end?


Does a love exist

Bright enough

To burn forever?

Love is strange

Because

One minute

You're wrapped in each other's arms

Begging

For every inch

Of their soul

To be both in you

And around you

But the next

You are whispering regrets

To yourself

I am spinning

Tired

Confused

My energy is escaping me

*Where am I?*

I scream it

But no one is there

No one.

I am alone


I did this


It was me


I chose this

Lost for breath

I can never take back

The way I gave you up

For nothing

Did I do this to myself

To see if I could?

Am I alone now because

In my bones

I feel it's what I deserve?

There has to be a reason

For all of this

Unless

I'm just perfect

At self-sabotage

Our lives become stories

It's strange sometimes to think

This

Will be mine

Terrifying

Is how it feels

Knowing

I left

So easily

When I promised

I'd stay


You didn't keep your promises, either

The pictures look

All the same

Empty shadows


You were there

And now you're not

In a weak moment

I might mistake loneliness

For regret

It must mean something

To feel

Like it was all

For nothing

Simple words

That tell us

How love

Is supposed to feel

Don't seem as simple

When you've lived them

Inside out

Sometimes an ending

Happens as quickly

As a shooting star

Only,

It's not nearly as beautiful

Just like I didn't mean to

I changed you

And just like I didn't want to

I changed, too

I *am* sorry for what happened

Something shifted

So slowly

It almost went unnoticed

But I should have listened

And told you sooner

Or maybe

I should have told myself

That is

How it goes

Sometimes

You drift

Apart

What would it be like

Reliving

Everything that is gone

Now that I know

How it ends?

I'll still

Always wonder

What she would have looked like

How her laugh would have sounded

If we loved each other long enough

To make her


*Our daughter*

If life had two doors

One for what we leave behind

Where you can see

How it would have been

If you never changed

And one for

How things will be

Because you did

I'd open the second

You say

You gave me your all

I agree

So much of you, in fact

That you're gone

Both from me

And from here

But mostly from yourself

I think you live there now

In the pit of my stomach

That's where I find you

Hiding

Every time

A dark shadow lived

Between the lines

Of you and me

When I open my eyes

I see all the ways

I've been keeping them shut

And staring

At all the fears

That live inside

My head

I tried to recall

The taste of you

When your love was still sweet

How could sensation evaporate

Into memory

No longer tangible

Now only imagined

I fumbled for you

To no avail

So I let go

And taste

Something new

Why hold

So tightly

To those

Who lost their grip on you

So easily

Fire leapt from my fingertips

Staying still no longer came easy

The choice to do right

Or be free

Was never fully clear

Watching cars

On the roof

My heart jumped

When I thought

Yours stopped

Where it could see me

Up here


Maybe I'm just feeling younger tonight

Is it possible

To go on

Forever

Never crossing paths

Again

As if

They were never meant to cross

At all?

I found out

Much too late

I did this for you

While you had done

Nothing

For me

And even though it doesn't matter

I realize

I was the fool

*A backbone*

*It's what we've been missing*

He stares at me,

*How can we stand?*

I ask him,

*How will we move?*

He replies,

*Our souls will do the moving*

But I remind him,

*Souls float*

You told me I'm like wildfire

That I'm burning us down

*No,* I told you

*I'm lighting us up*

Some days

I was so judged by you

Anything I did

Caused an earthquake

But you did so many things

And for me

It didn't even rain

But did you take the time to understand me?

Do you know how it feels

On the inside walls

Of my stomach?

Can you feel how quickly

And sometimes

Slowly

My heart beats?

Like how my cheeks

Have felt my tears

Or how my brain

Knows why they're falling?

He tells me

We are nothing

In so many words

But silently

He tells me

I am nothing

Pet names left your lips

Hopped off the tip of your tongue

Sweet like candy

*Baby,* you told me,

*You're mine*

It felt good

Until I knew

I am not to be had

I am to be admired

I'm the fool who listened

To your voice

Instead of my own

My belly shouting

The entire time

The truth of us

I always felt it

That quiet evil

Inside you

I could tell

By the way

They raised you

Despite your constant act

You were more than capable

Of being

Just like them


*Hateful*

I hear it

In my mind

The way they cringe

And wince

At my name

What has changed

Other than

Now they can do so

Freely?

The real warrior

Is the one

Who lets them talk

And believe

Whatever lies

Are being told

Because proving them wrong

Would require

Knocking down

Those doing the talking

Maybe I'm not done writing about you

And all the ways your charm

Hid your flaws

Like how you told me

I must have a brain tumor

When I said I didn't love you anymore

Because the week before that

You pushed me

And claimed I fell

How can I apologize for getting over you

When I told you what I needed

And you said

*That's just not me?*

What did you want me to do?

Be an actress

While my needs slowly faded away

Inside me?

I wonder if you know now

That was never the love

I deserve

A lover who

Eats up every moment

With me

Is a lover

I will keep


You were never that

Being alone

Feels a lot better

Without you

Finally

You aren't

Making me

This way

What good did you do here?

You left

And it still feels the same

More space, actually

Instead of less

*You'll never feel the same*

My mother told me,

*As you did about him*

I want to tell her now

*Mom,*

*I feel better*

It's been long enough now

That I can't remember

Anything but

Reasons why I was wrong

I used to see examples of love

In paintings and photographs

Lovers

Intertwined

So close

It confused me

I never wanted that from you

And that's how I know

Wanting to feel

Needed

Not by just anyone

But by a man

Who sets me on fire

When my light is dim

And even when I'm already burning

I need him to bask in my brightness

Simply because

He wants to

Falling for myself

More and more

Now that I realize

You never met this part of me

The comfort of sadness

I have always known

Became heavy enough today

To let it go

Moving on

Is a mix between

Empty

And free

But a little more free

Standing by the ocean

One of my favorite things

Funny

I like it better

Without you

When we met

I found my harbor

A ship that sailed too long

I was tired

About to sink

So I stayed, floated there

Content in your home

But baby,

I'm no ship

I am the water

I am my home

PART TWO

Runaway

**Coming up from dirt**

**I felt broken**

**Like I had climbed out of my own grave**

**Or maybe**

**That I was still climbing**

**I didn't yet realize**

**I was blooming**

**And that sometimes**

**Blooming hurts**

The first time I ran

I cleared my name

Here, I was new

It felt like

The sun

Was able to soak a little deeper

Into my skin

Now

Here I am again

With a new name to clear

And nowhere to run

Except back into

Myself

Sometimes I imagine

A sea of eyes

Staring down at me

Thinking

*Look at her,*

*Dreams too big*

*For such*

*A little girl*

Writing my insides out

Curious to hear

My own voice

Like fire

My fingertips

Have been begging

To do anything they can

To help

Engulfing

What's left of me

So all that remains

Pours out

Like rain

From the pressure

A new season is upon me

I find myself alone

Free

Yet terrified

I seek comfort

Probably in the wrong places

But isn't comfort

All the same?

There comes a point

Where life can make you feel

Lost

Utterly blind

To the way the whole thing works

Just when you thought

You knew

You find out

You don't

And that uncertainty

Becomes water

And drowns you

I sit with my feelings

Wondering

Which ones to trust

They've been known to lie

When I believed in them most

Fighting fear

Wondering

If it's fooling me

Ruining things

Like it always does

When it sneaks in

Unwanted

And unnecessary

My mind

Is so powerful

That is has

Created

And

Destroyed me

All at once

I feel hollow

Missing the piece of myself that makes me whole

My compass

Why love

Never feels complete

Is because I'm waiting

For you

To exist

And tie up

Every loose end

Letting go of an idea

Is sometimes harder

Than letting go

Of what is real

Setting my soul on fire

Deciding to carry on

Can't tell if I'm brighter for it

Or simply burning down

Our bodies

Can teach us

A thousand things

On a Sunday

 I learned

Being uncomfortable

And staying there

Helps us grow

But my heart taught me

There is an important difference

Between

Discomfort

And pain

Stay uncomfortable

Push through it

But always

Leave the pain

Pain

Is a signal

To move

First

Feel it

As a warning

Then run

*Fast*

Little fears bounce through my mind

Sharp as they stick

I never knew what it felt like

To be safe

What if I'm

Just one of those

Failure stories

Is my blind faith

In happiness

An illusion?

The funny thing about me

Is that I can't really tell

When I'm unhappy

Or just craving

Chaos

My life

Has me

Wrapped up

In vines

Some days

They are

A little

Too tight

Today

I've spent a lot of time

Wondering

If my feelings are chasing me

And if so,

Are they close?

When judgement comes

From your beginning

The very people

Who made you

How do you go on

Loving yourself

The same?

Who will ever love you fully

If they can't?

Face to face

With another hardship

I stand grounded

Strong

But now and then

I catch myself

Looking over my shoulder

Expecting no one

Almost as a reflex

And I'm right

Wisdom

Is earned

At a price so great

That those who have yet to afford it

Are only rich enough

To buy judgement

Place your trust

Carefully

They'll surprise you

And only if you're lucky

Will it be pleasantly

Down to my own name

I am vulnerable

My roots

Prove my weakness

Tied to me

In a clinging hold

Dying to hear them

Calling back my childhood

The only part I remember

Being sweet

If only my life had tasted

More like summer


*Loons*

Some nights

I can still feel her

The girl

Who grew up

Into me

Hasn't fully

Let go yet

When I was younger

I was so lost

I'm older now

And thought I was found

But I'm still

So far from home

Fill my life with souls

I've been alone too long

Even when I wasn't


*How I pray*

Could it be

That tears well up

From all the times

You were too strong

To cry?

All the times

It made sense

To hurt

But for some reason

You couldn't?

Is that why

Right now

I have no reason to cry

But the tears

Are begging

To pour?

Drowning myself

In distractions

Numbing

The parts of me

I don't want to meet

Again

Finding ways to be

More free

Less worried

Forces me

To let go of some things I love

Like control

Life

Isn't real

The way they tell it

Grab on

While you can

And let go

Just as often

If I could see

My breath

After I write

I'd be breathing out

Ghosts

Will these dreams

Teach me

What I'm dying to know

Awake?

The universe

Is funny

A joker

Who will always catch you

But leave you wondering

Just the same

My thoughts scatter

Dark places and possibilities fill my mind

Jumping like sparks

With the same intensity of heat

From thought to thought

Being haunted and reborn in the same moment

It feels

Irresistible

Like a circus but not as colorful

It's all a game in my mind

And I'm only playing it

A character in the circus

But not the leader

Because to be in control

I'd have to leave

And go to the quiet side

The place that always finds the right answer

It's simpler there – less heat, fewer dancing sparks

I've only heard about it, never actually reached it

Despite my endless travels

Somehow it sounds

Less alluring

What you want

And what is real

Are sometimes

Too different

To exist together

I have always been one

To love change

A stagnant life

Seems to drive me crazy

But these changes

Are taking a bit longer

To grab onto

Maybe I'm finally ready to hold on

Maybe I'm a little scared

They'll slip away

Am I strong

Or am I an actress

Dancing around ideas

Staying silent

Closing my eyes

Quieting my heart

*All the ways I hurt myself*

Scaring off

My own fear

Just as birds fly

When threatened

Wondering

What will it be

That jolts me awake

And sends me soaring

Back to safety

Will I ever make it

To a place

That doesn't hurt

After resting there a while?

And feels right enough

To be so still there

That I can

Settle?

Nothing feels worse

That needing to apologize

For who you are

And meaning it

Damaged women

Are like mirrors

To me

The things I don't feel

Are entirely clear

But I wish I knew

What I do feel

When night comes to greet me

I'm reminded

Of my mortality

As young and fragile

As it is

I'm truly just trying to get by

On the waves of joy

That splash up

And crash down

All too frequently

For my taste

Being alone becomes uncomfortable

It makes me wonder

If I like myself

At all

I have this gut feeling

That my gut is lying

Have you ever felt frozen

Where the only movement you make

Is caused

By melting

Blinded by uncertainty

Am I in danger

Or

Am I making it all up

*Consume too much,*

My captain said,

*And you'll die*

I laughed at him

I was starving

The hunger already killing me

So I ate

And ignored my captain

Who laughed as I perished

Sometimes

My ideas make me wonder

If I can trust myself

I drown in my thoughts

But the world gives me answers

It has to be real

I crave it

In the deepest parts of my mind

I need to fly to feel the wind

Not imagine it

*Is my strength a lie?*

I question it

My weakness seeps under the door

Threatens to drown me

Carry me away

On the back of my own wave

To a place

Where frauds live

*It's only fear,* I whisper

Soothing myself

*I'm still standing*

I carry my innocence on my back

Like a burden

Always feeling the need

To preserve it

As if a lack of experiences

Somehow makes me

Angelic

Constantly asked to describe

The things I haven't done

Instead of being recognized

For what I have

Why are women being preserved

As children?

We are not innocent

We are unstoppable

They say I'm just a runaway

The only way I have survived

But I'm not

I run at things

I'm still running

Closing my eyes

Feeling the wind under me

I can imagine how I'll fly

When I'm free

Towering through the sky

I remind myself

I am limitless

Flowers fall down around me

Circling me in love

As if a fresh new day

Was sent straight from my soul

To my aching body

Reminding me

I deserve nothing less

Than to be surrounded

By joy

In every direction

But always beginning

In the center

Even though

I'm walking under clouds

The sun is still there

Kissing my skin

I can feel it

Soon

It will come out

To greet me

Life tries to harden me

But I grow softer

Intentionally

My heart

Cries love

Enough to

Fill the ocean

Maybe it's not

Everything

But if I cared less

I wouldn't be me

I always have been

I just have to

Be


*My biggest secret*

Why are we made

To feel shame

When we ask for

What we want

From love?

I can't help it

That my heart beats stronger

Than average

That my mind gets wrapped up

In affection

Love is simply

What fills me

It is the one thing

That makes me believe

In joy

I revel in it

Do not focus

On what you deserve

From love

But instead

What your lover

Deserves

From you


*It will tell you everything*

You can't pretend

To have it all

Or settle

For the sake of comfort

You're letting life win

Run against the wind

Chase only yourself

The path they've made for us

Just isn't good enough

Your life

Will never stop thanking you

For setting it free

And listening

To every whisper

Both loud

And soft

It will

Surround you

In love

And beauty

Until you are unable to feel

Anything

But cradled

In your existence

I am a city

Vast

Seemingly endless

And beautiful

With dirt on my ground

And all the noise I make

My intense history

Each part illuminates me

And when my sun sets

I glow

The uglier part

Of growing

Has been the backbone in me

Becoming thicker

No longer does my skin

Smell of sugar

Now you have to get close enough

To taste it

In order to know

Just how sweet

It can be

My choices

Do not make me

Anything except

More alive

A little wiser

Perhaps older

They especially

Did not break me

I am whole

I like to be twisted

And broken

It's beautiful

Writing my fears away

Kills them instantly

I was afraid

Shedding my skin

Would leave me

Vulnerable

And alone

But

I am glowing

Home

Is a place

Where you can

Come to terms

With yourself

I write

When it's late

Because

Most beauty

Is made

In the dark

I know

It's right

Because

I'm afraid to die

Before it happens

When you find something

That sings to your heart

Like morning birds

Take it for yourself

Unapologetically

You are worth

Every word

You wish to speak

Escape to the place

Where love knows no bounds

And you can feel it

As much

As breathing deeply

Hold it there

And listen

If it feels anything

Like your breath

Stay


*If not, run*

Feeling beautiful

Reflects on our faces

Like sunshine

If my story

Were a painting

It would not be bright

But it would be

Beautiful

Like an ocean

Full of deep blues

That I have felt

In every shade

*Unbridled*

I will never rise from ashes

That would mean I had burnt out

# UNBRIDLED

# PART THREE

Ghosts

Is the sweet pink rush

In the beginning of love

Just a wave of chemicals

In our brains

Confusing us

Into believing

Another living soul

Could be a replacement

For what we have lost

Within ourselves?

I fell so hard

I disappeared

Thunder

That's what I feel

The only response I can think of

When they ask me

To describe it

Walking on a wire

Towards you

Falling

At your feet

When I land

Red in my cheeks

At the way I've been acting

Over you

Is your caution

Because we're so new?

Or do your moods

Change

Suddenly

All the time?

Some days

It's safe to fall in love with you

Other days

I'm terrified

Wondering

Will time change your senses?

Will you eventually feel secure?

I can't help myself

I am

Falling

Either way

Making sense of you

Is like unraveling

A necklace

That has been resting at the bottom

Of your mother's jewelry box

That she lost

When you were

Only a sparkle

In her eye

Are you more beautiful

For having been hurt?

I can smell the damage on you

And to me

It smells like home

I almost

Wish

You didn't burn

Quite as bright

As the sun

It makes

Everything

Other than you

Seem dimmer

When you leave

The room

Baby

We look so good on paper

Star-crossed lovers

Destined to meet

We even broke up two love stories

To be together

So you tell me, lover

What is this darkness I feel in the pit of my stomach?

Are we as toxic to each other

As we are to ourselves?

Dragging each other down

Like we always have

As individuals

Or could it be

We did meet for a reason

And the stars did align

So we could learn to be more tender

And love each other more gently

Just as we begin

To love ourselves

Why do I try so hard

To be more than comes natural

When I'm with you?

Is it guilt

Because I loved before

And failed?

Or are you really

That

Good

Struggling

To decide

If it's hurting me

To love so much

Should I step back

From my heart

And get to know

My mind?

With you

It feels like

I'm standing

In a wind tunnel

And you

Are the wind

*Can I ask you something?*

I said to him,

*Do I need to know too much?*

Pausing

I tell myself

Either the answer is no

Or it's none of his business

What I need

I know what you want

But I can't shine like the sun always

I'm a broken kid

Just like you

Will you

Always

Forget

That I still need

Sunshine

When it's cloudy?

It feels like

I taught you

I'm stronger

Than what's true

Sometimes

I want to wash you away

Like dirt off my skin

Watch you fall

So gracefully

Down to nowhere

As I see my skin brighten

I'm clean again

And you are somewhere

Spread out

Untraceable

But I can't wash you off

You've made a home in me

Why can't you sink deeper, baby?

Further into my skin

I want to keep you

But also be bright

I can't have both

If you stay here, lover

On the surface of me

Ease into me

Let me love you as deeply as we love with our bodies

Free you from the ghosts I see following you

Can you see them?

They scare me more than they scare you

But the ghosts won't leave until you can love without borders

Do you notice the house you built around yourself?

They live inside, too – the ghosts

It's safe there, I've been inside once or twice

But you barely leave

And the ghosts don't enjoy visitors

You built it so long ago

It's crumbling now

And you know that

Open the door, you must be lonely in there

The sun is calling you

And so am I

The two of us – one hidden, one running

Why don't we make it our house

And get to know those ghosts

Maybe they will teach us about ourselves

And we can finally feel

At home

It's you

Without the ghosts


*My ending*

I liked you

At first I wanted to

You made me feel

So incredibly

Alive

But now you scare me

Because I like more about you

Every

Single

Day

But what is it you like about me?

Like paper

You are perfect

Until you crumble

Strange

The way

You commit

And hide

So equally

I always said

You remind me of a mountain

As I fell asleep next to you

Strong and steady

I would imagine it

Lush, green pieces all throughout

White gleaming snow at the top

The sun high

And the shadows

Few

With small purple wildflowers placed

So perfectly

But

You look different now

They gray shades

Darker

Ever since the sun slowly snuck off

Behind you

I hope soon

I can paint you permanently

In the sun

Heart full

And tired

*Enough*

She said,

*It's your turn*

Before she crumbled

From the exhaustion

Of pleasing someone

Who didn't want

To be pleased

Tell me a thousand times

You love me

And I'll still deserve to hear it

Again

Fearing

The kind and easy love I've craved

Could never be love for me

After all

Does my own damage

Make you appear

Harder

And colder

Than you truly are?

I stay

Waiting for you

To admit you feel me

As much as I

Feel you

It wasn't enough

To write for you

When you felt small

In order for you

To do the same for me

Maybe that's my problem

Maybe I need someone to love me

The way I love you

Wanting you

To glisten

From kissing me

But knowing

You'd rather

Stay dry

To think

You can love someone more

Due to their absence

Is like saying

*Come here, baby*

*Stand in the shade for a while*

*You need a little sunshine*

Don't be fooled

My kindness is my greatest strength

So strong, in fact,

It can crush you

And it will

The intensity

Of my love

Is bone breaking

But it's not your bones

That break

That face

Your body

It calls me

Now some time has passed

I'm seeing your insides

As you explore mine

I'll admit

I'm surprised

And it's not pleasantly

You tell me the truth

Now and then

When you aren't afraid

But now and then

Will never be enough

That pain

I feel

In my chest

Is making me

Want

To forget you

Karma is a green monster

She found me today

I strangely enjoyed meeting her

Simply because

It felt good

Knowing she was real

And maybe

She'd come for you next

The shadows

Of your past

Haunt me

More than they haunt you

Just because

She wore out

Your patience

Doesn't mean

I don't deserve it

I think her lips

Red like berries

Stained mine

When you kissed me

I'm afraid you see her

When you look at me

And feel her

When we touch

She's on you

Like a shadow on the ground

A fog

Clouding it all

Darkening everything

Maybe when some time passes

And she is washed

Completely off

Your skin

You will feel

A little lighter

And I can love you

A little easier

I can't stop hearing

The echo of your words

Telling me

This was all

Just for fun

Especially since

Now

You're in my house

Throwing away my things

Making yourself

Just a little bit

Too comfortable

How can you let him convince you

That saying you are anything but

Magnificent

Is his form

Of flattery?

How can you let him stop you

From writing words that you feel

Because you would prefer

He not read them?

I wonder if it's only in my dreams

That the berry stain she left

Is fading

Off your lips

You could be

So soft

So beautiful

If you let go

Just a little bit

PART FOUR

Mountain

Like a mountain

Your edges are sharp

But I'll move over you

Like water

To help smooth them

People say

Love

Is dangerous

I never understood why

Until I met you

And tasted that fear

Suddenly

I was in love

And in danger

I could never deny you

Even on days

Me and you

Felt

Impossible

I wanted you anyway

We continue to be

Pulled together

Without explanation

A feeling

I never knew

Could be real

Questioning

How could this be real?

Why was I given

Exactly

What I wanted?

Waiting

For it to crumble

Because I'm scared

I don't deserve it

Like a sick joke

I'm terrified

You'll disappear

Something about you

Is harder

Both to understand

And to feel

Falling for you

Is slow

Messy

But

I think

Worth it

You feel familiar

And brain new

Like the rain

But isn't rain like that anyway?

Finding you

Has given my ideas

A place to fly

Because yours

Fly right along

With mine

You can't know

The relief

Now that they are no longer

Stuck in my chest

Beating with my heart

But no one else's

It makes me feel

Just a little more

Alive

I'm afraid

Of weakening

Under the spell

Your love

Has put on me

But then I remember

This love has made me

Stronger

From the beginning

Stubborn love

You can be so foolish

You are so much like me

You bring to life

The part of myself

That until now

Only I knew how to love

As we ran

We ran into ourselves

And I learned

Part of me

Also means you

Rising high

At the thought of you

Breathing deeper

When you're near

You caught me

In that sweet spot

Between broken

And whole

Girl

And woman

Teetering on the edge

I saw the way you looked at me

Your gaze

Bringing my strength

To the surface

The very idea

Of your admiration

Pushed me

Toward the light

Not because

I couldn't see it before

But simply

Because I saw how strong I could be

Next to you

If self-love is the answer

And you are just like me

Are you my answer?

It feels like summer coming around again

Even though it's at its end


*Something about him*

I wake up

To your affection

So tired

But you brighten me, always

Just another way

You are so kind

Did you know

I can feel you?

Just like I can feel fire

Right before

It burns out

I have to learn

To let you love me


I'm a fast learner

Take a look

Everything you ever wanted

Has ocean eyes

And they are looking

Right at you

Fears creep up inside

Like vines

Swallowing me whole

The intensity

Like flames

Until you're there

Soothing me

I still can't tell

If it was the lights of New York City

Or your eyes

That blinded me that night

Either way

I won't see things the same

Ever again

You say this isn't easy

Bad timing

But I wonder

Maybe it happened like this

So later

It can feel easy

Together

Strong

Like a mountain

With eyes

Like the ocean

It's no wonder I fell for you

When I relate your beauty

To nature itself

Your presence

Despite the fear

Makes me feel

Worth it

Almost more

Than if you had no fear at all

I was afraid

My fire would be

Too hot

But you walked through it

Like rain

I've never felt more beautiful

Than I do now

Standing at the edge of you

Ready to fall

When I lay still with you

My thoughts turn electric

I feel them

From the inside out

These moments have me bursting like a star

I'm in love

The way her nose

Sits just a bit

Differently

Her bone structure

Is what you'll remember her by

When age

Comes to stay

On her face

When her hair

Doesn't smell the same

As before

And her eyes

Don't burn as brightly

The way the sun

Catches her cheek bones

Will make you feel

Twenty-five again

When you smile

The energy could match

A thousand sunflowers

When the summer is new

So don't drift from that, baby

The thunder you create

With your sorrow

Will down them

Sometimes

People leave

But

You are magical

Love spilling from you

Like the river you are

Nevertheless

All the things

That made you tough

Left a piece

That I can love

Just a little deeper

Because of it

Forgive me

If I'm being too lighthearted

When you over analyze things

It just seems as if

I'm listening to myself worry

In the past

While I'm standing

Where it's clear

That everything will be

Just fine

Something as serious

As forever

Could never be

This easy

Maybe

You are just what I needed

I look at you

And wonder

How have I not found you

Sooner?

The way I'm drawn to you

Strong enough to turn tides

Why couldn't it have led me to you

First?

That star

Reminds me

Of you

So stay

Like it does

And shine

Like it is

Right now

Falling for you

Feels like magic

That I'm finally wise enough

To understand

Sink into me

So you can feel

What I feel

Let go of the fear

That you aren't better

Because better

Isn't good enough

To describe you

Words like

Undeniable

Magnetism

Right

Flood my mind

When I think of you,

Ocean Eyes

You are more

Than better

You are

Everything

A slight hint of dreams in your voice

Turning my head at the sound of it

You're just like me

I feel it most

Before I fall asleep

Wanting you to know

As the day slips away

I'm in love with you

But I stay quiet

Sitting in my thoughts

Uncomfortable, but sweet

This untouchable line between us

Begging to be crossed

The words burn in my belly

Dancing there

Like flames

Rising to the roof of my mouth

As we lay there

Together

Waiting

Things felt

So blurry

Until I met you

Now the pieces

That had no place

Have fallen

Exactly where they belong

And it all makes sense

Feeling free

All I've ever dreamt of

And here you are

Freeing me

I love you

So gently

A love I crave

For myself

Laying with you

I breathe you in

Feeling you

So still

You're like a mountain

You talk about pine trees

I think to myself

How lovely you are

That you love them

How simple that is

And how I love simple

Like the lines sunshine makes through a window

Us

Somewhere dancing in between

On the same line

Feel it

Be still

For this love

Is ours now

Desperate

To immortalize

The way I feel

Through writing

Can words ever be enough

To capture

How I'm blooming for you

As if you are the sun

After a night that threatened

Never to end

I'm grateful

For the days

That were good

But have gone

They help me savor

Every moment with you

Taking in

Every inch

Of your smile

And every tone

Of your voice

The butterflies you give me

That I had stopped believing in

And all the dreams I have

Of what can be

A woman falling in love

Is a powerful thing

Like waves

Baby

You make me whole

I've never known a love so full

Even before it has fully blossomed

I long await

Watching it bloom

You surprised me

I didn't expect you

It started with the way you looked in my direction

As if I was

The eighth wonder of the world

Before I even knew

You meant it

Followed by words

That warmed me

To my very core

Then

You handed me a mirror

To help me see myself again

And here you are now

My home

It's been strange

To know someone

So similar to myself

It shows exactly

How electric

My thoughts can be

And how excessive

My worries are

In a way

It's charming

Our minds

Ever parallel

Are amazing

I'm meeting myself now

As a woman

Letting go

Of the girl

I used to be

And I'm so glad

You're here

To meet me, too

Drifting into sleep

Beautiful, strong, alone

Makes me love

Sleeping

Next to you

Even more

Funny how we fell in love

In the spring

You feel

Just like fresh air

When the world gave me

You

Everything was beautiful

Everything was new

I don't see you first

When I close my eyes

I see something beautiful

And it reminds me of you

It's fitting

That the story of us

Is just as messy

As the stories

We have

Of ourselves

Maybe now

We can write

A new one

I was right

When I called you a mountain

Looking out at them now

You are just as beautiful

Opening

Like a flower

Exploring

My own petals

Learning myself

As I learn you

Maybe

I couldn't have loved you

The same

If I didn't

Love

Before you

And fail

Signs

Falling at my feet

Just as you

Have fallen into my life

Feeling still

Something

I've never believed in

Until you made each moment

Worth pausing for

I love you like

I imagine

The moon feels

About a favorite star

That one

In particular

Shining brighter than the others

Always catching my gaze

In a simple place

Surrounded by simple things

Nature

And

Each other

I knew you would be all my things

And more

Our love is like spring

When you first notice

The flowers have bloomed

Despite the lingering winter

Together

We observe

Love is beautiful

And blooming

Even

In the cold

Is there a sweeter taste

Than your lover's skin

On your lips

Five minutes after

I love you because

You are always singing

Under your breath

And there's not much better

Than the sound of your voice

To fill the quiet with

Those words sounded so sweet

In our kitchen that morning

I never knew I could fly

Until that day

How can I love you so much

That even the little things about you

Are my best case scenario

I don't think I could love you more

Than I do in this moment

But then I do

Every time


*Things I've said out loud*

Choosing my words

In a powerful way

Has shown me the strength

Of language

How love can be spilled

From both the body

And the tongue

Still –

It's best to do both

At the same time

You listen to me

The way I listen

To wind in the trees

During a storm


Thank you for that

The sun kisses us

As we find each other

Waking, slowly

A new day washes over me and you

Our words are gentle

The air is new

This is what perfect feels like

Across from me

Ocean Eyes

Saying all the ways he loves me

Through them

Where we realized

We make sense

Where we chose

To face our fears

Where we decided

Against judgement

Where I think

We fell in love


*Portland*

I see us there

Endlessly happy

Letting the water lull us to sleep

Awaking with the city

Together

Our chance

To build what we've craved

But have never had ourselves

Will it finally

Reach us?

A quiet rush of silence

Fills me up with calm


We're going home

The way you love cartoons

And mornings with me


The fact that your eyes look like the sun

Shining into the ocean


How you've known a life like mine

And we're both a little broken


Your beautiful mind

That bounces seamlessly between humor and insight


The way you sat and read *The Little Prince* for me

And wondered, as I did,

If I would tame you


How the universe has been in on this

All along

And all the proof it has given us


How I crave your body as much

As you crave mine

The way it felt to kiss you that night

At the overlook

While we listened to French music

For the first time


All the times we could have been an almost

But the universe refused

And so did we


You make me feel like anywhere

Could be home

With you


All the little things

Made falling

So easy


And here I am

Unexpectedly

In love

With you

Climbing felt

Endless

But here you are

At the top

Maria K Crawford is a dreamer, a lover, and a romantic. Growing up in Illinois, Maria moved to New York City at eighteen and has been searching for home ever since. Many of the poems in *Unbridled* were inspired by the city of Portland, Maine, where Maria lived at the time of publishing. As Maria studies to become a psychotherapist, she uses poetry as a way to reach not only her own heart, but the hearts of others. As she continues to live outside the lines, Maria is thrilled to welcome you into her world through words.

www.mariakcrawford.com

*About the author*

Made in the USA
Columbia, SC
30 November 2020